A New True Book

THE PACIFIC OCEAN

By Susan Heinrichs

CHILDRENS PRESS®

CHICAGO

Pacific coastline near Elk, California

Dedicated to Annie

Library of Congress Cataloging-in-Publication Data

Heinrichs, Susan.
  The Pacific Ocean.

  (A New true book)
  Includes index.
  Summary: Specifically discussing the Pacific Ocean,
provides basic information about the sea, including
wave formation, currents, tides, marine biology, and
the landscape of the ocean floor.
  1. Pacific Ocean—Juvenile literature. [1. Pacific
Ocean. 2. Ocean] !. Title.
GC771.H44 1986   551.46'5   86-9653
ISBN 0-516-01295-9

PHOTO CREDITS
Root Resources:
© Kenneth W. Fink—2
© Louise K. Broman—40 (top)
© Ben Goldstein—40 (bottom left)

Historical Pictures Service—6 (left),

Granger Collection—6 (right)

© Cameramann International, Ltd.—10
(2 photos), 27 (right), 28 (right)

© Photri—11 (left), 18, 27 (left)

© Bob and Ira Spring—11 (right),

Odyssey Productions, Chicago:
© Charles Seaborn—12, 30 (right), 36 (right)

Journalism Services, Inc—13

Tom Stack & Associates:
© Dave Baird—16,
© Mickey Gibson—28 (left)
© Tom Stack—29, 36 (left)
© Neil G. McDaniel—30 (left)
© Ed Robinson—32 (left), 37 (2 photos)
© Gary Milburn—38 (top and bottom right)
© A. Kerstitch—32 (right)
© Carl Roessler—35, 44 (left)
© Gerald Corsi—40 (bottom right)
© M. P. Kahl—42 (right)
© Brian Parker—Cover

Scripps Institute of Oceanography—21
(2 photos)

Department of the Navy—25

H. Armstrong Roberts, Inc:
© A. Foley—33

Valan Photos:
© Paul L. Janosi—38 (bottom left)

Gartman Agency: 45
Christy Volpe—42 (left)

James P. Rowan—44 (right)

Maps—Albert R. Mangus, 4, 7, 9, 14, 22,
33 (right)

Cover: Waikiki Beach, Honolulu,
      Hawaii

TABLE OF CONTENTS

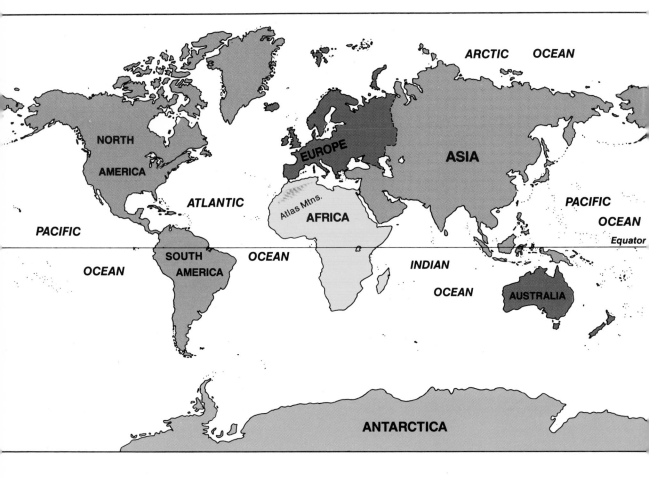

4

THE BIGGEST OF ALL

Someone gave our planet the wrong name. Anything called "Earth" should be covered with soil. But our Earth is covered mostly with water. And the biggest body of water on Earth is the Pacific Ocean.

The world's biggest ocean was not even discovered by Europeans until the year 1513. That

Balboa (above) discovered the Pacific Ocean. Ferdinand Magellan (right) was the leader of the first sea voyage around the world.

year, Vasco Núñez de Balboa from Spain climbed a high mountain in Central America. There he spotted a large body of water. Balboa named it the South Sea.

In 1519, Ferdinand Magellan sailed to this

6

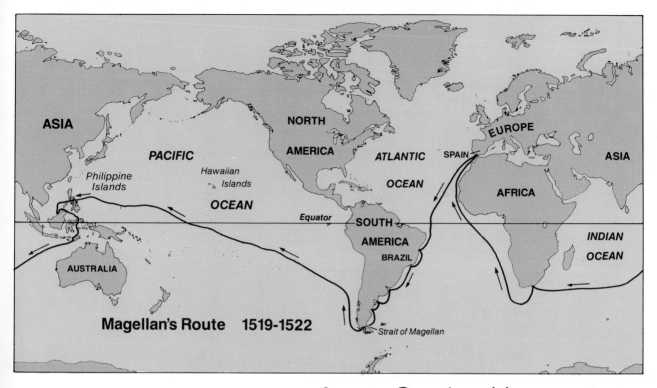

Magellan's Route   1519-1522

new ocean from Spain. He
planned to sail around the
world. His trip dragged on
for months. His ships ran
out of food. The sailors
had to eat leather and
sawdust. But the waters
Balboa had called the

South Sea were calm. Magellan called the sea *mare pacifico,* meaning the peaceful sea. Magellan died before the trip was over. His men sailed across every ocean and back to Spain. They were the first to sail across the Pacific Ocean and around the entire earth.

Much later in 1768, Captain James Cook from England explored the Pacific islands. He took

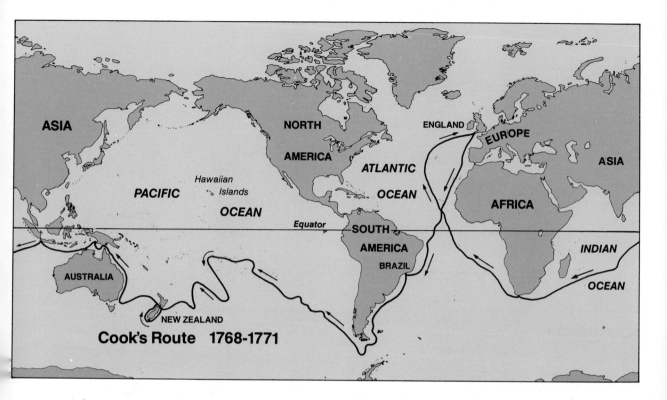

ASIA

NORTH
AMERICA

ENGLAND

EUROPE

ASIA

ATLANTIC

PACIFIC

Hawaiian
Islands

OCEAN

AFRICA

OCEAN

Equator

SOUTH
AMERICA

INDIAN

BRAZIL

AUSTRALIA

OCEAN

NEW ZEALAND

Cook's Route   1768-1771

scientists with him to study
the plants and animals
they found. He made maps.
In fact, Captain Cook did
more than any other
person in history to change
the map of the world.

THE WATER'S EDGE

The shore is where an ocean meets the land. Some places have shores made of sand and bits of shells. Sandy shores are called beaches.

People often search along ocean beaches for

Beaches in the Marshall Islands (left) and Honolulu (right)

Rocky coastline in Oregon (left)
and Washington (above)

shells and other things that
wash up. Once in a while
they find pieces of fishing
nets from across the
ocean.

In other places, there is
no shore. Steep cliffs drop
straight down into the
water.

Rock oysters

Hard-shelled animals like snails and oysters live along the rocks at the bottom of the cliffs. They get their food when water splashes on them. Then they clamp themselves shut to keep from drying out.

THE OCEAN IN MOTION

The Pacific Ocean holds
the most water of any ocean.
However, the water doesn't
just sit there. Somehow
it's always moving.

Wind can move the
water. It whips the surface

Surfer rides the waves.

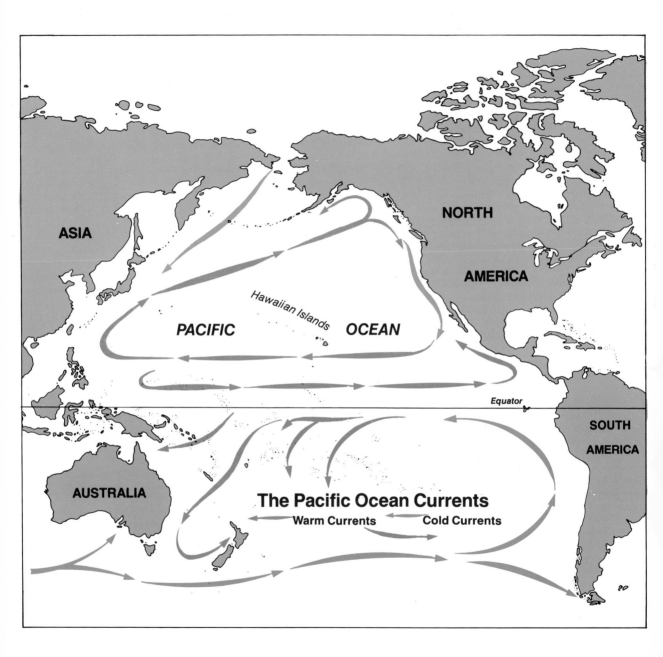

The Pacific Ocean Currents

Warm Currents   Cold Currents

waters into waves. In some places, wind and the earth's rotation work together to swirl the water around. These water movements are called currents.

The currents in the Pacific Ocean follow a circular pattern. In the Northern Hemisphere they move in a clockwise pattern. In the Southern Hemisphere they move counterclockwise.

Mud flat at low tide

The whole ocean can
move at once. Twice a day
the water creeps slowly up
the shores. Each time it
stops and slowly creeps
back again. This slow
movement of the whole
ocean is called the tide.

People used to think tides were caused by the earth trying to breathe. But the ocean waters move that way because they are pulled by gravity of the sun and moon.

Even the smallest bits of water have motion. These droplets are called water molecules. They are too small for the naked eye to see. But millions and millions of tiny molecules are sloshing around in the ocean.

Some molecules on the surface evaporate into the sky and gather as clouds. Then they rain on the land. There they flow into rivers and head back to the ocean.

All these droplets have been moving around the Pacific Ocean since the world began. You probably drank water molecules that once were on the other side of the world. Or maybe you ate a bowl of soup containing water molecules that once fell as raindrops upon dinosaurs.

THE SECRET LANDSCAPE

The bottom of the ocean is called its floor. Until around 1920, the ocean floor was thought to be flat. Then scientists discovered a way of "looking" at the floor by using sound.

They sent sound waves down to the ocean floor. Some sounds bounced back quickly. They had not traveled far to get down and back. Scientists knew

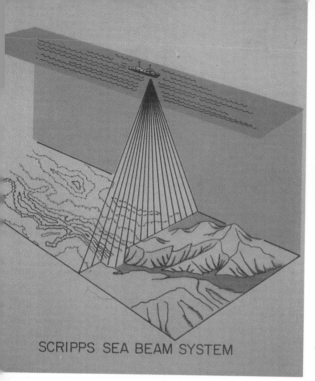

SCRIPPS SEA BEAM SYSTEM

Research vessel *Thomas Washington* (above) was built for the Scripps Institution of Oceanography at the University of California. Carrying 17 scientists and a crew of 25, this ship can stay at sea for four-week periods. Using Sea Beam (left), the scientists mapped this section of the ocean floor that was 11,220 feet below the surface about 1,800 miles east of Tahiti. The string of volcanoes (shown in red) reach heights of 690 feet. The craters (shown in blue) reach depths of 158 feet.

the ocean floor was rather close at this point.

Other sounds took a long time to bounce back. Scientists figured the floor underneath was far away. Finding depths this way is called echo sounding.

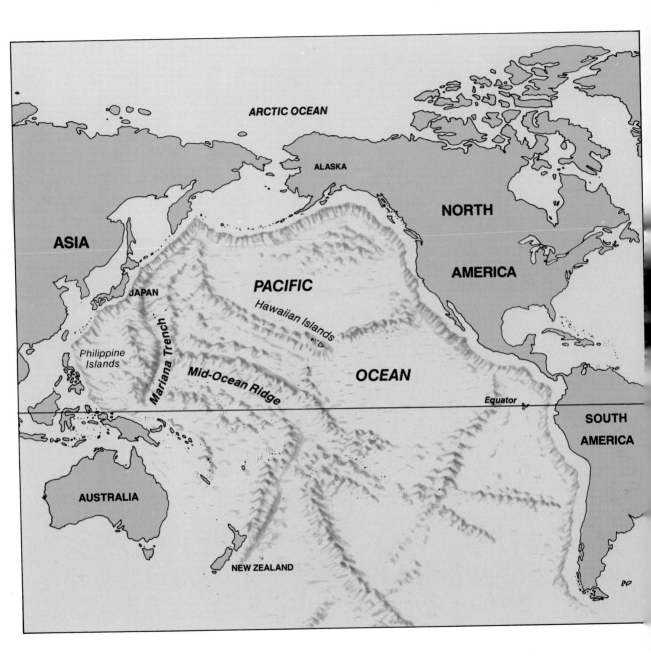

ARCTIC OCEAN

ALASKA

NORTH

ASIA

AMERICA

JAPAN

PACIFIC

Hawaiian Islands

Mariana Trench

Philippine
Islands

Mid-Ocean Ridge

OCEAN

Equator

SOUTH
AMERICA

AUSTRALIA

NEW ZEALAND

As it turned out, the ocean floor wasn't flat at all. A string of huge mountains, called the Mid-Ocean Ridge, rises from it. The ridge winds its way through every ocean in the world. But its tallest mountains are found in the Pacific Ocean.

The deep cracks in the floor are called trenches. The Mariana Trench in the Pacific Ocean is the deepest. Its bottom is seven miles down.

One morning in 1960, two men climbed into a special vessel called a bathyscaphe. As they went deeper into the Mariana Trench they saw fewer and fewer animals. The water grew dark. At 1,000 feet it was completely black. At 4,200 feet, the bathyscaphe sprang a leak. A few minutes later it stopped.

Finally, the men hit bottom. They switched on a light and looked outside. The water was icy cold

Bathyscaphe
Trieste

and completely dark. But they saw a fish living at that great depth!

The men stayed on the bottom for about twenty minutes. Then they started back up. This was the deepest anyone had ever gone into the ocean.

BLACK SAND BEACHES

Along some parts of the sea floor there are volcanoes. Volcanoes are mountains which formed when gas and melted rock shot out from deep inside the earth.

Most volcanoes no longer spew rock or gas. Many underwater volcanoes are so deep no one has ever seen them. Others stick out of the water.

The Needle (left) on Maui
Volcanic island in Tahiti (right)

The Pacific Ocean has
thousands of volcanic
islands.

The islands of Hawaii
are part of a string of
volcanoes. There are
hundreds of volcanoes in

the string. Only a few poke out of the water.

Islands and mountains formed from volcanoes are solid black. The rocks are black. The soil is black. Even the sand on beaches is black!

Black sand beaches are found in Hawaii and Tahiti

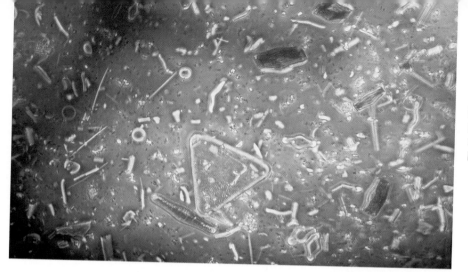

Marine diatoms, a type of plankton, magnified one hundred times

TINY CREATURES

Sunlight shines on the top layer of the ocean. Tiny plants smaller than pinheads live in the ocean's top layer and grow in the sunlight. Tiny animals also live there. They eat the plants.

These little plants and

animals are called plankton.
Plankton gets pushed and
moved around by the water.

Another animal that gets
pushed around is the
jellyfish. Some jellyfish are
smaller than a penny.
Others are as big as an
umbrella.

Jellyfish

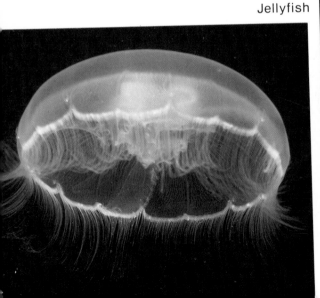

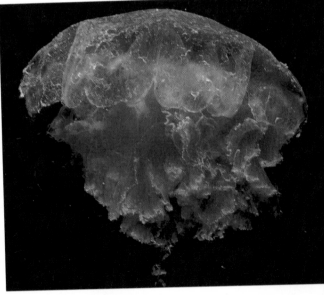

A GREAT REEF

Not all smaller animals
are easy to move like the
plankton. Some glue
themselves to the ocean
floor or to something hard.
Others attach themselves
to fish and get around that
way. Still others stick to
each other. Tiny animals
called coral do this.

The coral animal really
has a soft body. But it
builds a hard crusty cup to

Coral

live in. Another coral
animal can attach its cup
to the first one.

There is a place close
to Australia where coral
animals have been sticking
themselves to each other
for years and years.
Together the corals are a

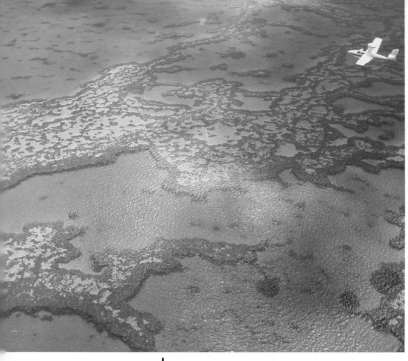

Great Barrier Reef,
Australia

huge mass over a thousand miles long. Any large mass of coral is called a reef.

The coral near Australia is named the Great Barrier Reef. It is famous as the largest mass in the world built by animals.

TRICKSTERS OF THE DEEP

In the ocean, bigger fish eat little fish. So little fish have ways of keeping safe by fooling their enemies.

In the Pacific Ocean there is a fish called the butterfly fish. It has a pair of small eyes. Near its tail it has large spots that look like eyes.

Big fish come up to a butterfly fish and see those big eye-spots. They snap

Butterfly fish

at what they think is its
head. But they only get a
mouthful of water. The
butterfly fish darts away.

Big fish can be tricky
too. The stonefish is a
large fish that lives near
the Great Barrier Reef. It is
lumpy, warty, and shaped
like a rock. Its body is

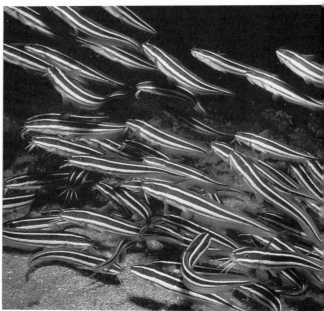

Stonefish (left) and
sea catfish (right)

covered with pieces of
skin that wave in the
water like weeds.

Small fish do not notice
the stonefish. They swim
right by. Then the stonefish
opens its huge mouth very
fast. The small fish are
sucked in.

Coral reef (left) and
white-tip reef shark (above)

Many other fish make
their homes on a reef.
There are catfish with
whiskers. Whiskers feel
and taste food before it's
eaten.

There are carpet sharks
that spread themselves flat.
They pretend to be part of
the ocean floor.

Giant Pacific octopus (above), giant
clam (below left), and kelp (below right)

In other areas of the ocean, there are some huge plants and animals. The giant kelp plant grows in cooler parts of the Pacific. Sailors have found kelp blades over 600 feet long.

The giant clams may weigh 500 pounds. Giant octopuses are over 130 pounds. They swim in the northwest Pacific.

Western gulls (above), American oyster
catcher (below left), and blue foot boobies (below right)

OCEAN BIRDS

There are many different kinds of ocean birds. Each has something special that helps it get food.

Oyster catchers are birds that live along the shores of North America. They have long razor-sharp bills to pry shells apart. Then they feed on the soft animals inside.

Penguins are chubby birds that like colder waters. Their wings are too

Humboldt penguin (right) and Adelie penquin (far right)

short and stubby for flying.
Penguins swim after their
food. Their wings make
great fins.

Penguin feathers are
coated with oil. The oil
helps them slip through
the water extra fast.

TOO MANY QUESTIONS

We still know very little about the huge Pacific Ocean. Most study has been at the ocean's surface. That is because it is easy to reach. The ocean floor is hidden under many tons of dark, icy water.

There are still many questions to be answered. How many volcanoes are down there? How can fish

Reefs and islands (above) in Palau, Micronesia. Seacoast in Ecola State Park, Oregon.

live at the bottom of a trench? How come the tons of water above does not crush them? How long did it take to build the Great Barrier Reef? And

does the butterfly fish *ever* get caught?

Scientists have many more questions than they have answers. Maybe someday you'll discover some of these answers.

WORDS YOU SHOULD KNOW

bathyscaphe(BATH •ih •skafe) — a specially made ship used to explore the ocean's depths

beach(BEECH) — a sandy shore of an ocean or other body of water

clamp(KLAMP) — to fasten two parts together so they are very tight

cliff(KLIF) — a very steep section of rock that drops from land directly into water, without any shore

currents(KURR • untz) — water movements in a large body of water that are caused by wind and the earth's rotation

evaporate(ih •VAP •uh •rate) — to change from liquid to a gas, or vapor

fin(FIHN) — a skinlike part of a fish or other water animal; used to guide the animal's movements

gravity(GRAV • uh •tee) — the moving attraction of the sun, moon, or one of the planets on things, such as water, on the surface of another body

molecules(MAHL • ih • kyools) — the very tiniest bit of something, made of atoms, that still has all of the properties of that something

oceans(OH • shunz) — the largest bodies of salt water on the earth

reef(REEF) — a large mass of rocks or coral animals that have stuck their crusty cuplike homes together

shore(SHORE) — the place where an ocean or other body of water meets the land

tide(TEYED) — slow, twice-a-day movement of water up a shore and then back down again

trench(TRENCH) — long, deep crack in the ocean floor

volcano(vahl • KAY • no) — a mountain formed when gas and melted rock shoot out from deep inside the earth

INDEX

About the author

   Susan Heinrichs holds a Master of Science degree in zoology with a specialty in aquatic biology, and studied marine biology at Duke University Marine Research Lab. Her articles have appeared in several scientific journals. As a consultant to the U.S. Army Corps of Engineers, she formulated environmental impact statements and researched zooplankton species in man-made lakes. Her research activities at the National Reservoir Research Center have included investigating trout kills on Arkansas rivers and coordinating research and data on reservoirs nationwide.

   Ms. Heinrichs has taught general and aquatic biology, human anatomy and physiology, and animation at the Universities of Arkansas and Oklahoma. A photographer, electron microscopist, and scientific illustrator, she has published illustrations in numerous journals. She currently owns her own graphic arts business in Norman, Oklahoma, and is directing and shooting instructional video tapes for electron microscopy students.